Understanding Regional
Cooperation in Asia Book Series

Echoes of Wisdom: Chinese and ASEAN Proverbs across Cultures

Series Editors: Lu Guangsheng and Feng Yue
Editors: Feng Yue and Wang Rong

Understanding Regional Cooperation in Asia Book Series
Echoes of Wisdom: Chinese and ASEAN Proverbs across Cultures

Series Editors: Lu Guangsheng and Feng Yue
Editors: Feng Yue and Wang Rong

First published in 2025 by Royal Collins Publishing Group Inc.
Groupe Publication Royal Collins Inc.
550-555 boul. René-Lévesque O Montréal (Québec) H2Z1B1 Canada

Original edition © Yunnan Education Publishing House

All rights reserved. Without limiting the rights under copyright reserved above, no part of this publication may be reproduced, stored in or introduced into a retrieval system, or transmitted in any form or by any means (electronic, mechanical, photocopying, recording, or otherwise), without the prior written permission of both the copyright owner and the above publisher of this book.

ISBN: 978-1-4878-1297-3

To find out more about our publications, please visit www.royalcollins.com.

Echoes of Wisdom: Chinese and ASEAN Proverbs across Cultures

www.royalcollins.com

Contents

Foreword — vii

Preface — xi

1 — 1
One Flower Does Not Make Spring,
but a Hundred Flowers in Bloom Bring Spring
to the Garden

2 — 29
Mutual Respect Is Precious as a Treasure

3 — 55
The People Are the Foundation of the Nation;
When the Foundation Is Strong, the Nation Is
Peaceful

4 **77**
Forging Iron Requires a Strong Hammer

5 **101**
Many Hands Make Light Work;
Many Stakes Make a Strong Fence

Conclusion **125**

References **127**

Foreword

Proverbs Resonate, Echoing Support for Proposals

Proverbs, as succinct and widely circulated expressions of folk wisdom, are collectively created by the people. These artistic phrases encapsulate the richness of popular wisdom and universal experience. Their simplicity and precision enable them to convey profound ideas in a refined linguistic form, making them favorites among national leaders and great writers for expressing their sentiments and ideas.

President Xi Jinping frequently uses proverbs from various countries and regions in his important speeches, articles, and messages both domestically and internationally. His unique linguistic style and charm resonate widely with people from different nations. These proverbs, akin to the nourishing rain of spring, capture the hearts of people worldwide, demonstrating respect for diverse civilizations and showcasing exceptional diplomatic wisdom. During the high-level dialogue between the Communist Party of China (CPC) and world political parties in March 2023, the General Secretary of the CPC Central Committee and President Xi Jinping proposed the Global Civilization Initiative, which advocates for "respecting the diversity of world civilizations," "promoting shared human values," "emphasizing the inheritance and innovation of civilizations," and "strengthening international cultural exchanges and cooperation." Proverbs, as ideal carriers of cultural exchange and mutual understanding, play a vital role in promoting the acceptance and implementation of this initiative globally.

In his keynote speech at the Boao Forum for Asia Annual Conference 2015, President Xi Jinping stated: "Friends from Southeast Asia say, 'When the water rises, the lotus flowers grow higher.' Friends from Africa say, 'If you want to go fast, go alone; if you want to go far, go together.' Friends from Europe say, 'A single tree cannot block the cold wind.' The Chinese say, 'When the big river is full, the small rivers are full; when the small rivers are full, the big river is full.' These all express the same principle: only through cooperation and mutual benefit can we accomplish great, good, and lasting endeavors. We must abandon the old mindset of zero-sum games and you-win-I-lose thinking and embrace a new concept of win-win cooperation, considering others' interests while pursuing our own and promoting common development while seeking our own growth." These proverbs from different regions all emphasize the importance of unity and cooperation for development.

Similarly, during his state visit to Vietnam, President Xi Jinping published a signed article titled "Working Together to Create a Better Future for China-Vietnam Relations" in the Vietnamese newspaper *Nhân Dân*. The article noted: "There is a Vietnamese proverb that says, 'One tree does not make a forest; three trees together make a mountain.' I look forward to having in-depth discussions with Vietnamese leaders during my visit to plan the future direction of China-Vietnam relations, ensuring their steady and long-term development. I believe that as long as China and Vietnam work together and strengthen cooperation, we will create a better future for our relations and achieve mutual development and prosperity." A single Vietnamese proverb vividly portrays the comradeship and brotherhood between China and Vietnam.

Proverbs encompass a wide range of subjects, from kings and generals to common folk, from astronomy and geography to daily life, and from moral philosophy to practical wisdom. They can be humorous, satirical, or vividly descriptive, encapsulating people's judgments of life and their aspirations. Through continuous refinement over long periods, proverbs have become increasingly polished, showcasing the brilliance of language and leaving a lasting impression.

The people of ASEAN countries, like the Chinese, enjoy using proverbs to express their thoughts and emotions. These proverbs reflect rich local characteristics, using common local knowledge and unique local flora and fauna as metaphors. Due to frequent folk interactions and cultural exchanges, these proverbs also exhibit strong cultural commonalities, expressing universally recognized values in simple language.

China and ASEAN countries are good neighbors, friends, and partners, connected by mountains and rivers. They share similar civilizational values and mutual respect. The common values of humanity are the natural outcome of the development and progress of human society at a certain stage, akin to plants rooted in the soil of various countries, thriving in different historical, cultural, ethnic, and social environments. Finding the right path to recognize, learn from, understand, tolerate, and respect different civilizations is crucial to advancing the building of a community with shared future for humanity.

Over the past thirty years since China and ASEAN established dialogue relations, they have journeyed through an extraordinary path. During this period, economic globalization has deepened, and the international landscape has undergone profound changes. China and ASEAN have moved past the shadows of the Cold War, jointly maintaining regional stability, leading East Asian economic integration, and promoting regional development and prosperity.

Today, the establishment of the China–ASEAN Comprehensive Strategic Partnership injects new impetus into regional and global peace, stability, and prosperity. Respecting the pursuit of common human values by the peoples of all countries, practicing genuine multilateralism, and ensuring that international and regional affairs are handled through consultation to meet the region's practical needs, align with the global development trend, and fulfill the aspirations and hopes of the people.

Through the proverbs of China and ASEAN countries, we can appreciate the rich and diverse civilizations and the shared values and vivid truths they contain. Let us start from our land and jointly promote the implementation of the Global Civilization Initiative, advancing the long-standing tradition of friendship between China and ASEAN into a new era.

Preface

From the vast sea of proverbs across ASEAN countries, we observe that people from these nations share a common pursuit of universal human values such as peace, development, fairness, justice, democracy, and freedom. The ancient civilizations of the East have, through proverbs, provided wise and vivid summaries of the characteristics of human society in colorful and varied languages. For instance, there are Malaysian proverb, "Different fields have different grasshoppers," Thai proverbs, "Good ginnabar needs no paint to be red" and "Hands not rowing, rather feet blocking the water," and Singaporean proverb, "If you are not upright, you mislead others." These proverbs, rooted in everyday life experiences, convey profound truths and provoke deep reflection.

Proverbs are products of the historical and cultural contexts of various nations, representing the practical and experiential wisdom of working people who gained over long periods of social production and life. They are characterized by their simplicity and spontaneity. Although some proverbs may be influenced by their historical context and may exhibit a certain degree of partiality, this does not detract from their ability to reflect deep truths about civilization, culture, and shared human values.

These proverbs, rich in content, cover all aspects of production and life. They articulate universal human values from multiple perspectives, levels, and fields in a grounded and relatable language. They possess a deep historical and cultural heritage, offer cautionary and guiding significance for the present, and are simple, easy to understand, learn, and remember, filled with the essence of everyday life.

When understanding, knowing, and disseminating these proverbs, we must also analyze and interpret them using Marxist positions, viewpoints, and methods. The report of the 20th National Congress of the CPC emphasizes, "To uphold and develop Marxism, it must be integrated with the excellent traditional culture of China. Only by rooting in the fertile soil of our nation's history and culture can the tree of Marxist truth grow deep and flourish." This underscores the significant value and role of China's excellent traditional culture in the persistence and development of Marxism. Proverbs are an important part of a nation's culture, vividly reflecting the culture and the civilization formed on its basis. Chinese proverbs reflect China's excellent traditional culture and the values of the Chinese people, forming an integral part of Chinese civilization.

Promoting the proverbs of China and ASEAN countries not only helps us understand and interpret the views on civilization and development from a civilizational perspective but also facilitates mutual cultural exchanges between China and ASEAN countries. It allows us to tell the Chinese stories well and gain a deeper understanding of the history, culture, customs, and traditions of ASEAN countries.

1

One Flower Does Not Make Spring, but a Hundred Flowers in Bloom Bring Spring to the Garden

Introduction

President Xi Jinping, in his Global Civilization Initiative, remarked: "'One flower does not make spring, but a hundred flowers in bloom bring spring to the garden.' In today's world, where the destinies of nations are closely intertwined, the coexistence and mutual learning of different civilizations play an irreplaceable role in advancing human society's modernization and enriching the diverse garden of world civilizations." Eastern civilizations boast a long, splendid history and a rich tapestry of content. Within this broader framework, each country, region, and ethnic group exhibits unique characteristics, contributing to the diversity of the global civilization garden.

The 20th National Congress of the CPC proposed the comprehensive advancement of the great rejuvenation of the Chinese nation through Chinese-style modernization. This modernization is characterized by a large population, common prosperity for all, the harmonious coexistence of material and spiritual civilization, harmony between humanity and nature, and a path of peaceful development. It is a modernization that is rooted in China's national conditions, drawing on the experiences of other countries, inheriting historical culture, integrating modern civilization, benefiting the Chinese people, and promoting global common development. It is both the broad avenue for building a strong nation and national rejuvenation, and the essential path for China to seek human progress and a harmonious world.

China respects the development paths chosen by ASEAN countries and other regions, emphasizing equality among nations, regardless of size or strength. It opposes bullying and advocates for mutual development. Like China, ASEAN countries have experienced invasion and oppression by Western powers in modern history, making them particularly cherish the hard-won peace and development of today. Looking to the future, we must be well-prepared, consolidate our greatest strategic advantages, inherit and promote Chinese civilization, achieve the great rejuvenation of the Chinese nation, and unite with the peoples of the world, including ASEAN countries, to build a community with shared future for humanity.

One Flower Does Not Make Spring, but a Hundred Flowers in Bloom Bring Spring to the Garden

一花独放不是春，百花齐放春满园

China

When only one flower blooms, it cannot be called spring. When a hundred flowers bloom, the garden is vibrant, and this is the true essence of spring. Spring is a wonderful season of growth and harmony, a time of joy and peace. People love spring, but it cannot be defined by a single, exceptional flower. It requires a myriad of colors and various forms of flowers blooming together to create a flourishing garden.

This proverb is rich in philosophy: on one hand, it elucidates the relationship between the whole and its parts. "One flower" represents a part, while "a hundred flowers" symbolizes the whole. The function of the part must be realized within the whole. On the other hand, "one flower" and "a hundred flowers" are interconnected, emphasizing the need to respect the diversity of the parts, thereby respecting the diversity of different cultures. Additionally, the blooming of a hundred flowers in spring is an inevitable event, aligning with the trend of historical development.

If the world had only one type of flower, no matter how beautiful, it would be monotonous. Whether it is Chinese civilization or other civilizations in the world, they are all human creations. Promoting cultural exchange and mutual learning enriches human civilization, allowing people to enjoy a more meaningful spiritual life and create a future with more choices.

"One flower does not make spring, but a hundred flowers in bloom bring spring to the garden" originates from the ancient Chinese text *Ancient and Modern Virtues* (古今贤文). President Xi Jinping mentioned this proverb in his keynote speech, "Working Together to Create a Better Future for Asia and the World," at the Boao Forum for Asia Annual Conference 2013 and in his 2014 speech at UNESCO headquarters, conveying its profound meaning.

Shoes Fit Only When You Wear Them

鞋子合不合脚,自己穿了才知道

China

Shoes are worn on one's own feet. Whether they are too big or too small, too wide or too narrow, soft or hard, or comfortable or uncomfortable, only the person wearing the shoes knows best.

People have summarized this truth from their daily life experiences. Although it is simple and straightforward, it reveals a profound truth. It is often used to describe the suitability of marriages, families, careers, and personal life experiences. A similar expression is "As one drinks water, one knows best whether it is cold or warm."

In 2013, during his visit to Russia, President Xi Jinping said in his speech at the Moscow State Institute of International Relations: "We advocate that all countries and peoples should enjoy dignity together. We must uphold equality among countries, regardless of size, strength, or wealth, respect the right of all peoples to choose their own development paths, oppose interference in other countries' internal affairs, and uphold international fairness and justice. 'Shoes fit only when you wear them.' Whether a country's development path is suitable can only be judged by its own people."

From everyday life to international relations, we must respect others' choices. Each country has its own historical traditions, current conditions, and cultural backgrounds. Choosing a path that suits oneself is the best.

The paths of development vary and there is no single model or standard. Development paths are reflected in specific indicators such as economic growth levels, the acquisition of political rights by the people, the protection of ecological rights, and the improvement of people's livelihoods. For ordinary people, the most direct reflection is the level and progress of living standards, and they have the most say in this.

The Inequality of Things Is Their Reality

物之不齐，物之情也

China

The myriad differences among things in the world are their inherent reality and objective law. There are no two identical leaves on a tree, nor are there two identical grains of sand in a desert. Everything in the world has its own unique form and existence. Given this, we cannot judge things by a single standard or measure gains and losses with the same yardstick.

This phrase comes from the ancient Chinese text *Mencius · The Writings of Teng Wen Gong (Part I)* (孟子·滕文公上): "The inequality of things is their reality. Some are twice as good, some ten times, some a hundred times, and some a thousand times. To compare them to one another is to bring disorder to the world. Would people make the same price for big and small shoes? If so, they would all be faking it, and how could they manage the state?"

President Xi Jinping quoted this phrase in his 2014 speech at UNESCO headquarters and again in his speech at the Boao Forum for Asia Annual Conference 2015. These references express the Chinese leadership's respect for the various forms of civilizations and their advocacy for cultural exchange and mutual learning.

A Perfect Match Like the *Xiao* and the Flute

配合得像箫和笛子

Thailand

The harmonious and fitting duet of the *xiao* (箫, a bamboo wind instrument) and the flute can produce the most beautiful melodies. The Thai people are fond of singing and dancing and have a deep love for music. They often use locally available bamboo to create various instruments, with the *xiao* and the flute being the most common.

In Thailand, there are two types of *xiao*: one used to accompany dance, which has seven sound holes and produces a melodious and lyrical tone with a pastoral flavor; the other is used to accompany martial arts, with eight sound holes—six in front and two in back—producing a robust and rich sound, similar in timbre to the Chinese *suona* (唢呐, a Chinese traditional double-reed woodwind instrument).

Thai bamboo flutes come in three sizes: large, medium, and small, with the medium size being the most frequently used. The flute has seven finger holes and one membrane hole. Air is blown through a reed fixed at one end of the bamboo flute; directly facing the reed is a rectangular sound hole with thin edges at the back of the flute. There are three main forms of instrumental ensembles in Thailand, each with large, medium, and small combinations. In small ensembles, only a few basic instruments are used; medium ensembles include most main instruments along with some special-function instruments; large ensembles usually feature pairs of various instruments.

Only harmonious ensembles can bring about aesthetic enjoyment. For the Thai people, the perfect match between the *xiao* and the flute, with their complementary high and low tones, provides a unique artistic pleasure in life.

In the Land of the One-Eyed, Follow the One-Eyed

到独眼的地方要跟着独眼

Thailand

When a person arrives in any place, they must adapt to the customs of that place.

The myth of the one-eyed person is a common early legend in many regions worldwide, including the Chinese *Classic of Mountains and Seas* (山海经), which also mentions "one-eyed people."

China and ASEAN countries are diverse in terms of ethnicity and culture. Through long histories of interaction, a tradition and mutual understanding of respecting the customs and habits of different ethnic groups in various countries and regions have formed—sing the songs of the mountains you are in and respect the culture of the people you visit.

Thus, the Thai proverb, "In the land of the one-eyed, follow the one-eyed," emphasizes respecting local customs. Similar sayings include "Enter through the small door, exit through the main gate" and "Bring a knife when entering the forest, and remember the way out," all conveying the need to adhere to local customs and to be thoughtful and careful in actions.

Sleep Face Down When on High; Sleep Face Up When on Low

睡在高处要俯卧，睡在低处要仰卧

Thailand

This is a metaphor. When one is in a high position, he should look down; when in a low position, he should look up. In Thai culture, this means that superiors should care for their subordinates, while subordinates should obey their superiors.

In daily life, Thai people emphasize the order of seniority, respect, and hierarchy. For instance, when the juniors are with the elders, they must not be higher than the elders and should walk behind them, bowing and lowering their heads. This proverb, based on Thailand's traditional view of order, emphasizes mutual understanding and respect between different social strata.

The ancient Chinese politician, thinker, and writer Fan Zhongyan wrote in his "Record of Yueyang Tower" (岳阳楼记): "When he is in high office, he will worry for the people; when far he is from court, he will worry for the ruler," meaning that officials should care for the people when in office and worry for the ruler when not. This is similar in spirit to the Thai proverb.

Every society has its systems and norms to maintain harmonious functioning. In social life, everyone must consider others' perspectives and positions, respect each other, and work together in unity. This approach ensures the success of endeavors, regardless of status or power. "Sleep face down when on high; sleep face up when on low" conveys Thailand's philosophy of social governance in simple terms.

Everyone Has Their Own Preferences

各有各的爱好

Thailand

Different people have different preferences, and different groups have different cultures. Recognizing the differences between people is the premise of mutual respect.

Some like swimming, and some prefer running; some enjoy eating meat, while others are vegetarians; some love spring, and others prefer autumn. In Thailand, someone might take a day off school to help their parents with work, while another might go to a temple to earn merit because they dreamt their deceased grandmother wanted porridge. As long as such choices do not harm others, they are considered legitimate.

Influenced by Buddhist culture, Thailand values harmony and has a high degree of cultural tolerance. In 2021, Thailand made the Chinese Spring Festival a public holiday. Festivals are a reflection of a country's or a nation's traditional culture, distinguishing it from others and showcasing its unique cultural charm. The inclusivity of festival culture also reflects the historical background and attitude of accepting different national cultures. Thailand's recognition and attention to Chinese festivals is a manifestation of this cultural inclusivity.

"Radishes and greens, each has its preference." The world becomes a vibrant place only with diversity and variety.

Reap the Fruits of the Tree You Tend

吃哪棵树的果, 围哪棵树的园

Vietnam

Every task comes with specific responsibilities and duties. Whatever benefits one receives, they must pay a corresponding price for them, ensuring a stable and harmonious society.

In Vietnamese society, for every right a person has, there is an emphasis on corresponding duties. This is encapsulated in the proverb "Reap the fruits of the tree you tend"—if you enjoy the fruits of a tree, you must take care of the tree. Rights and duties are seen as equal; what is a right or duty for one person is a corresponding duty or right for another. This cultural tradition is pragmatic and rule-conscious, protecting the common interests of people and ultimately becoming a consensus in Vietnamese society.

There are many similar sayings in Vietnam, such as "Those who have lamps will light them," "Each rows their own boat," and "Eat the offerings of a Buddha, burn incense for that Buddha." These proverbs use different metaphors and life scenarios to illustrate that whatever one receives, one should give something in return; reaping is predicated on sowing. Clear delineation of functions promotes fairness more effectively than unilateral giving or receiving.

Two Leaders in One Family; Two Monarchs in One Nation

一家两主不和，一国两君不安

Vietnam

This Vietnamese proverb expresses an understanding of democracy and cultural tradition, emphasizing both respect for differences and the importance of unified decisions. A good head of a family or a national leader can unite the people, serve them, and bring stability and unity to the country.

Vietnam has a long history of a feudal society. During times of war and prolonged struggle, Vietnam developed a highly efficient and centralized political system with a significant impact. In the governance system, there must be both democracy and centralization, creatively transforming and innovatively developing democracy and centralization based on the country's traditional culture. This path leads to a better future for the nation.

One Field with Two Irrigation Ditches, One County with Two Chiefs, and One Family with Two Sons-in-Law Are Not Good

一块田有两条水沟、一个县有两个县长、一个家有两个女婿不好

Laos

In Laos, even though there are many capable and thoughtful people who can serve the public, it is widely believed that governance should be the responsibility of an individual. This Lao proverb uses a field to illustrate this concept. If a field has two irrigation ditches, it can easily become flooded during storms, causing losses for the villagers. Similarly, if a county has two chiefs, their differing personalities, thoughts, and abilities could lead to competition and division. Likewise, a family with two sons-in-law would face many problems.

A House without Windbreaks Will Be Penetrated by Crows

房子没有防风板，乌鸦就要飞穿过

Laos

Laos has experienced multiple dynasties, each with different governance characteristics, resulting in a diverse social system. However, the expectations and demands of the people for national leaders have shown similarities across different periods.

"A house without windbreaks will be penetrated by crows" signifies that a good leader is like a windbreak, protecting the people from external threats. Similar proverbs are common in Laos, such as "Without stakes, the fence lets in animals" and "Good rice needs irrigation ditches." These sayings use everyday items to illustrate the importance of national leaders. Without good leaders to guide the people in building their homeland, the country cannot prosper. Thus, a nation's high officials or top leaders must be capable and loving, and contribute positively to the nation. A country must be governed by brave, capable, and thoughtful leaders who act as walls against enemies.

Lao proverbs are distilled from life experiences and are considered cultural heritage. Lao scholar Rasani Sothikun once said, "In-depth research of proverbs allows us to feel the guiding principles of national leadership in different eras." Proverbs are not only moral teachings in Lao society but also reflect the people's thoughts, life experiences, and cultural customs.

When Three Elephants Clash, the Sky Collapses

三头大象相撞，天都要塌

Laos

In Lao life, elephants are very important companions. They often symbolize powerful individuals and groups. The perception of elephants as "strong" and "capable" translates into corresponding metaphorical imagery in language. The close relationship between people and elephants has led to the creation of many succinct proverbs, such as "Seeing an elephant defecate, one imitates" to describe putting on a false front and "Riding an elephant to catch a grasshopper" to denote making a big deal out of a small matter.

If powerful "elephants" are in conflict and do not cooperate, causing disputes without anyone to mediate, the resulting strife and division within the group can lead to disaster for the people.

A Cloth with Four Corners Should Not Be Used as a Bag

四角的布匹，不要拿来做背包

Laos

This proverb describes the need for focus and specialization in tasks. Things or people with too many entangled interests are not suited for important responsibilities. Using a simple, common item from daily life, this proverb concisely encapsulates the worldview and methodology of the Lao people, highlighting the principles and guidelines necessary for completing a task.

The Lao people generally practice Buddhism, leading peaceful life where everyone performs their respective duties. Although society has different strata, the country respects and protects the people's right to be masters of their own destiny, emphasizing reliance on the people's strength for their well-being and happiness.

A Golden Swan Does Not Fly behind an Eagle

金色天鹅，不会在老鹰背后飞

Laos

Laos is primarily mountainous with abundant tropical flora and fauna, so the locals often use animals and plants as metaphors. They liken the followers of a leader to eagles and the leader to a golden swan. "A golden swan does not fly behind an eagle" means that a leader must take the lead, serving as an example and a guiding force for the people.

This Lao proverb suggests that leaders must be at the forefront. Regardless of the circumstances, leaders must lead the people, embodying noble qualities, possessing convincing virtues, and earning the genuine support of the populace.

The Fast Rabbit Crosses Three Ridges; the Slow Turtle Swims Three Lakes

快兔越三岭，慢龟游三湖

Laos

This proverb uses the characteristics of "rabbit" and "turtle" to illustrate that everything in the world has its strengths and uniqueness. The swift rabbit runs and jumps among the hills, while the slow turtle leisurely swims in the lakes. Different species live in different worlds, without the need for comparison or judgment. A harmonious world should embrace diversity and different ways of life.

The same applies to national political systems and democratic institutions. Different cultural backgrounds and social environments require different forms of democracy. True democracy should foster the spirit of democracy through bilateral and multilateral dialogues, establish a correct view of democracy, and reveal the true nature of any self-centered or superior "democracy."

This proverb uses the contrast between speed—fast and slow—and the common animals, rabbits and turtles, to reflect the essence of things from both sides. The form is balanced and harmonious, while the content is oppositional yet unified, possessing both expressiveness and persuasiveness.

If Everyone Got His Wish, the World Would Fall Apart

如果世界上每人都能如愿以偿，那这个世界必定分崩离析

Laos

In traditional Lao culture, the collective mindset is highly influential, similar to the values found in China, Vietnam, and other countries.

The Lao society is mainly influenced by Buddhism, Brahmanism, and indigenous religions, impacting various aspects such as art, thought, and customs, deeply affecting the Lao people's production and life. The Buddhist concepts of karma, compassion, restraint, and moderation discipline people's behavior; Brahmanism's theories of divine kingship have a long history; and indigenous beliefs instill a reverence for nature and ancestors, guiding people's actions. Together, they contribute to maintaining societal harmony in Laos.

The Lao people are gentle and kind, understand how to restrain their desires, and do not envy others' achievements; they seek happiness through labor and effort. This Lao proverb advocates the value of harmony.

Better to Love Your Own Home than Envy Others'

与其羡慕别人家，不如喜欢自己家

Laos

This simple and straightforward proverb expresses the basic attitude of the Lao people in foreign interactions—rather than admiring others' lives, it's better to appreciate what you have, as there is always something worth cherishing. It is similar to the Chinese saying, "Cherish your own broom," but with subtle differences.

Every country has its own dignity and value. From individuals and families to nations and regions, everyone has the right and freedom to choose their own culture and traditions and adhere to their values. While mutual learning and borrowing are encouraged, coercion to abandon one's home or culture in favor of another should not occur. Even if others' homes are good, people can still love their own homes. This represents respect, stability, and confidence.

Different Fields Have Different Grasshoppers

不同的田里有不同的蚱蜢

Malaysia

This Malaysian proverb illustrates that different environments yield different outcomes. Countries have unique conditions, cultures, and development paths, resulting in diverse democratic models. Indonesia's "Pancasila" and the democratic wisdom infused with "Asian values" in Singapore and Malaysia are examples of countries forging their own democratic paths through their development experiences. The construction of a democratic system must align with a country's conditions and the fundamental interests of its people. Whether a country is democratic should ultimately be judged by its people, and only democracy deeply rooted in a country's soil can truly bring happiness to its people.

In his speech at the UN headquarters in Geneva on January 18, 2017, President Xi Jinping quoted the saying, "The beauty of a dish lies in its harmony of different flavors," explaining, "There are over 200 countries and regions, 2,500 ethnic groups, and various religions in the world. Different histories and national conditions, ethnic groups, and customs have given birth to diverse civilizations, making the world more colorful. Civilizations are not superior or inferior, only different in characteristics and regions. Civilizational differences should not be a source of conflict but rather a driver of human progress."

The Chinese pursuit of "appreciating one's own beauty and that of others, and achieving harmony and unity in diversity" is embodied in the spirit of this proverb. This inclusive spirit is also a way to resolve cultural conflicts and achieve harmonious civilizations.

On the Same Bamboo Pole, Each Node Is Different

在同一根竹竿上，各节可各不相同

Cambodia

This ancient Cambodian proverb uses a simple life metaphor to explain the fundamental principles of cultural diversity and the building of a community with shared future for humanity.

Democracy is a concept centered on equality that emerges at a certain stage of human social development. As history progresses, democracy continues to be enriched by theorists around the world, forming different systems. The world's various civilizations have their own characteristics and shortcomings. Civilization is equal; there is no hierarchy of superiority or inferiority. For human society to advance, it must respect and preserve diverse civilizations, promoting mutual learning among them.

Just as a bamboo pole has different nodes, each country has complex realities, with its own culture and civilization, independent social forms, and governance systems. However, all live on the same planet and should jointly care for their shared home, respecting each other, seeking common ground while reserving differences, and pursuing common development. This aligns with the essential requirements and significant content of Chinese-style modernization as proposed in the 20th National Congress report, which advocates for "building a community with shared future for humanity and creating new forms of human civilization."

2

Mutual Respect Is Precious as a Treasure

Introduction

In China, equality is reflected in all aspects and links, and this equality is realized through the whole-process people's democracy. From the political process perspective, whole-process people's democracy tightly connects and integrates all aspects of democratic election, consultation, decision-making, management, and supervision, creating a comprehensive, full-chain democracy. Whole-process people's democracy effectively avoids the situation where people only have the right to vote but lack broad participation rights, preventing promises made during elections from becoming meaningless afterward. China insists on placing significant public decisions concerning national and people's livelihood within the democratic sphere for comprehensive consideration. At every level, major public decisions follow democratic procedures, undergo democratic deliberation, and result from scientific and democratic decision-making. These procedures typically include hearings, consultations, forums, and online inquiries, widely incorporating grassroots public opinion into the public decision-making process. Broad and orderly participation by the people is the essence of whole-process people's democracy and a critical measure of democratic quality.

In terms of party relations, the system of multi-party cooperation and political consultation under the leadership of the CPC is a fundamental political system in China. This new type of party system, created by the CPC based on the theory of the united front, emerged from China's democratic revolution process and is the inevitable result of historical development. In this system, the CPC is in a leading position, and the other democratic parties are its partners, forming a relationship between the ruling party and participating parties. The CPC and other democratic parties, along with patriotic individuals, discuss and consult on major national policies and important issues related to the people's interests, fully promoting democracy, achieving consensus through consultation, pooling wisdom, and mutually supervising each other, thus making decision-making more democratic and scientific. This party system and political structure embody the people's mastery of their own affairs, rooted in the fundamental interests of the people.

The advantage of China's multi-party cooperation and political consultation system lies in its ability to achieve broad democratic participation, reflecting various demands and opinions, while also realizing centralized and unified governance, enhancing efficiency. It prevents one-party dictatorship and lack of supervision while avoiding the political chaos and inefficiency caused by multi-party strife and mutual constraints. China's new type of party system has three novel advantages: representing the people's interests collectively and fundamentally; fostering cooperative and allied relations among parties; and ensuring democratic and scientific decision-making through institutionalized, procedural, and standardized arrangements, concentrating various opinions and suggestions to promote scientific and democratic decision-making.

This reflects China's emphasis on discussing matters widely, discussing matters well, and doing things through consultation. These concepts are embodied in China's political system and social life and benefit the people. ASEAN countries also have many proverbs reflecting the pursuit of equality, consultation, unity, and narrowing differences. These proverbs play a crucial role in their histories and promote national development and the realization of people's interests.

Pull Your Foot out of the Mud, but Words Once Spoken Can't Be Taken Back

脚陷进泥里拔得出，话说过头收不回

Myanmar

This proverb emphasizes the importance of not speaking excessively and maintaining appropriate discretion. If your foot gets stuck in the mud, you can pull it out without significant harm, but if you say something overly harsh, it can cause emotional damage that is hard to retract and difficult to remedy. Myanmar is a country with many ethnic groups and diverse cultures, and in daily life, people must pay attention to mutual respect and be mindful of their words to avoid causing irreparable harm.

Though proverbs are often short, typically consisting of a single sentence, they are powerful in conveying profound truths. They embody collective wisdom, oral traditions, and the people's perspective, reflecting the lives, thoughts, emotions, desires, and demands of ordinary working people. With healthy and positive mainstream values, proverbs deeply resonate with the pursuit of justice and good qualities, embodying a strong democratic spirit and creating a sense of kinship among people from different regions.

Every Cow Goes to Its Own Pen

谁家的牛进谁家的圈

Thailand

Like China, Thailand has a long history of agricultural development, with cows being crucial tools for farming. Thus, cows hold significant importance in Thailand, naturally leading to the creation of many cow-related proverbs.

"Every cow goes to its own pen" means that actions have consequences. In the past, cows were often herded together, and each cow would naturally return to its own pen. This proverb is commonly used to illustrate that good deeds yield good rewards, while bad deeds result in bad consequences.

In Thailand, people also use the saying "wheel and axle of the ox-cart" to indicate that good actions receive good outcomes. Influenced by Buddhist culture, Thai society believes in karma and the cycle of cause and effect. This belief in reaping what you sow extends to international politics, where Thailand values peace and handles international affairs with equal consultation and communication.

Bringing Sand into the Temple

搬沙入寺

Thailand

This proverb reflects an important ritual of the Songkran Festival in Thailand, where people bring sand from outside into the temple and build sand pagodas. Historically, Thai temples did not have cement or brick floors, and people entering and leaving the temple would take the sand outside, reducing the sand within the temple. During the Songkran Festival, people bring sand back into the temple as an act of merit-making and virtue accumulation.

The shared purpose of bringing sand into the temple is to perform good deeds for society and contribute to the collective. This proverb embodies the Buddhist teachings within Thai folk customs, encouraging people to do good deeds, cooperate for the collective good, and cultivate a high regard for public interests, fostering a sense of unity.

Don't Take the Fire from Your House Outside; Don't Bring the Fire from Outside into Your House

家里的火不要拿出去，外面的火不要拿进来

Thailand

This proverb means that family matters should not be aired outside, and external matters should not be discussed at home. Though it pertains to family relationships, it can also apply to international affairs, emphasizing respect for national sovereignty and non-interference in internal affairs. In diplomatic relations, upholding the principle of sovereign equality and mutual respect for sovereignty is both a right and a duty. Adhering to this principle is essential for building global peace.

Live in Harmony with All Neighbors and Avoid Gossip

和所有的邻居和睦相处，不说闲话

Thailand

Thai people believe that neighbors are the first to offer help in times of need, so they should support and not slander each other. This ethos of friendly neighborliness influences Thailand's approach to international relations, promoting peace and minimizing conflicts with neighboring countries.

Chinese culture also values neighborly relations, as reflected in the saying, "Distant relatives are not as helpful as close neighbors." China and Southeast Asian countries share geographical proximity and cultural similarities, making them "good neighbors who cannot be moved away." By living in harmony and resisting outside provocation, neighboring countries can pursue regional prosperity and development together, building a harmonious relationship.

The Village above Comes to Help; the Village below Comes to Assist

上边的村回来帮，下边的村回来助

Vietnam

This proverb means that if a village faces significant issues, neighboring villagers will come to help, reflecting Vietnam's agricultural tradition of mutual aid. In China's Zhuang ethnic areas, similar sayings such as "A single thread cannot weave a cloth; a single person cannot build a house" and "No family's roof is leakproof; no family's father is eternal" convey the same messages. In traditional agricultural societies, mutual assistance was a common practice in farming, harvesting, building houses, and during weddings and funerals. This proverb teaches the importance of solidarity and helping each other.

Don't Stop Rowing Because of High Waves

莫见浪头高，放下手中桨

Vietnam

This Vietnamese proverb means that when a boat is sailing on the water, if you stop rowing because of the rough waves ahead, the boat will either be swallowed by the waves or remain stationary. The proverb implies that only by persevering and overcoming difficulties can one reach a glorious destination.

On November 9, 2017, on the eve of his state visit to Vietnam, the General Secretary of the CPC Central Committee and President Xi Jinping published a signed article in *Nhân Dân* titled "Opening a New Chapter in China-Vietnam Friendship." The article quoted this Vietnamese proverb, stating: "As good neighbors, friends, comrades, and partners with interconnected destinies, we must maintain and develop our bilateral relations, assisting each other in maintaining stability, deepening reforms, and improving livelihoods, thereby advancing the socialist cause and promoting regional peace, stability, and open development."

China and Vietnam are close neighbors with interlinked destinies. The Chinese saying "a narrow strip of water" perfectly encapsulates their relationship.

Mutual Respect Is Precious as a Treasure

相互尊重,贵如瑰宝

Laos

This Lao proverb emphasizes the importance of mutual respect. In international affairs, all countries, regardless of size, should enjoy equal sovereignty. The United Nations Charter advocates resolving disputes by peaceful means, avoiding threats or use of force, and non-interference in any country's internal affairs. These principles form the core of modern international law.

Mutual respect is a key prerequisite for avoiding big powers bullying smaller or poorer nations. Countries should interact with each other on an equal footing, using inclusive, humble, and understanding attitudes to learn about each other, rather than demeaning others with arrogance and prejudice. Mutual respect is essential to eliminate power politics and hegemony, making it a concept as valuable as a treasure.

Making Friends Is Easy, but Keeping Friendship Is Hard

结交朋友易，保持友情难

Laos

This proverb highlights the importance of sincerity in maintaining long-term friendships.

The phrase, "It's easy to meet but hard to live together," reflects a common phenomenon in relationships. The Chinese saying, "Distance tests a horse's strength; time reveals a person's heart," similarly suggests that friendships, kinship, and neighborly relations require time and mutual understanding to build trust and maintain feelings.

When dealing with important development issues between nations, friction and conflicts can arise. In international relations, one must engage sincerely and emotionally, exchanging hearts rather than just interests. Only by genuinely considering friends' perspectives and thinking deeply about their development can friendships endure and flourish.

Sharing a Meal at the Same Table, and Eating the Same Piece of Fish

同吃一桌饭,同吃一块鱼

Laos

This proverb signifies the rarity and value of harmonious, close, and cooperative relationships. In Laos, sharing a meal at the same table and eating the same piece of fish are considered rare and precious bonds. Similar expressions include "sharing a bunch of bananas" and "sharing a banana blossom," all of which convey the value of friendship based on mutual support and integration.

Even a Tall Elephant Can Be Defeated by Small Ants

高高大象死于小小蚂蚁,这样的事也会发生

Laos

This proverb uses common Lao animals, elephants and ants, to illustrate that tyrants do not have a good end, and that weak individuals can unite to defeat strong enemies. In international affairs, powerful countries that bully smaller nations must be aware of the strong collective power of weaker nations uniting against them. Historically, China has advocated that the strong should not oppress the weak and the rich should not insult the poor. Regardless of a nation's strength, it is crucial to uphold mutual respect and solve issues through consultation to avoid harm to both sides.

A Bright Moon Alone Cannot Shine without Stars

一轮明月独放光，众星不围不显亮

Laos

Even a bright moon needs the surrounding stars to highlight its brilliance; a beautiful lotus needs the green leaves as a backdrop. Nothing can exist in isolation while maintaining its precious value. One must recognize and value the importance of seemingly insignificant companions.

In international relations, unilateral actions that infringe on the rights of other nations and ignore the equal, interdependent relationship between countries can lead to tension and disaster. "One fence needs three stakes; one hero needs three helpers" embodies the path to harmony through interdependence and mutual support.

A Person Is Valued for His Word; an Elephant for Its Tusk

人重其言，象取其牙

Cambodia

This Cambodian proverb uses the preciousness of ivory to emphasize the importance of a person's words. People must honor their promises and value their spoken words, treating others with honesty and sincerity. Another Cambodian saying, "Trust is like a tree," likens trust between people to a deeply rooted, flourishing tree. Both the tree and the ivory symbolize the value of trust and integrity.

China and Cambodia are close friends with a long-standing friendship that has withstood the test of time and changing international dynamics. Sihanouk once said, "The long-standing solid friendship between Cambodia and China is like an everlasting flower, always blooming under clear skies." This deep friendship is built on mutual trust and honesty in handling bilateral relations.

Even an Elephant with Four Feet Can Slip

大象有四只脚,亦有失足时

Cambodia

This proverb means that even a large and stable elephant with four pillar-like legs can stumble, implying that even the strongest entities can make mistakes or encounter difficulties. It serves as a reminder to remain vigilant and avoid complacency due to one's strength.

Humility and caution are valuable traits. Chinese sayings like "Sail with caution to ensure a long journey," "Heaven has rain, and people have misfortune," and "No one is perfect" all remind people to act carefully and avoid arrogance, thus preventing significant errors.

When Seeing Others' Mistakes, Do Not Gloat; When Praised, Do Not Become Conceited

见人错,勿幸灾乐祸;被人捧,勿得意忘形

Cambodia

This proverb advises correct self and others' perception. When witnessing others' mistakes, one should not feel happy but instead remind himself. When praised, one should remain clear-headed and not forget his true self. Maintaining integrity and calmness helps establish good social relationships, achieving equality, friendship, and mutual assistance.

In international affairs, developed and developing countries must help and understand each other, developing together without gloating over others' difficulties or becoming overbearing due to having many followers.

Do Good and Receive Good; Do Evil and Receive Evil

与人为善得以善报，与人为恶得以恶报

Myanmar

Influenced by Buddhist culture, Myanmar believes in karma and the cycle of good and evil, advising people to "perform all good deeds" and "avoid all evil deeds." The Chinese sayings, "Good is rewarded with good, evil with evil," "You reap what you sow," and "Do good, though unseen, and misfortune will be distant; do evil, though unseen, and fortune will be distant" convey similar ideas. Thai proverbs like "Good people are protected by ghosts, and bad people do not die well" also reflect this universal cultural concept.

As close neighbors, China and Myanmar share many similar cultural values. Whether through civil assistance or official aid, these cultural values are the foundation for deep friendships between nations.

Seedlings That Withstand Trampling Grow Strong; Those Who Endure Criticism Grow Wise

经得起践踏的禾苗壮实,经得起批评的人聪明

Myanmar

The Myanmar people believe that only seedlings that endure hardships can grow strong, and only those who accept criticism can improve and gain wisdom.

In the decision-making and management process, those who can widely listen to opinions and reflect the people's will can gain the people's support. Active and proactive participation in elections, consultations, decision-making, and supervision in social and political governance enables a brighter and better world. By working together, building mechanisms together, creating benefits together, and sharing interests, nations and peoples can embark on a path of prosperity and strength. Facing difficulties, not fearing adversity, and listening to critical opinions can make one stronger, thus better equipped to tackle challenges with courage.

Gain Knowledge through Intellectual Exchanges; Get Injured through Physical Fights

与人斗智得到学识，与人比武得到伤痛

Indonesia

This proverb emphasizes resolving issues through peaceful and friendly negotiations rather than advocating violence and conflict, which can harm both sides. In handling international affairs, the value of peace should be cherished to avoid the disasters that armed conflicts bring to regions and nations. Countries should respect sovereignty, engage in equal consultations, unite, cooperate, and learn from each other's wisdom and experiences, rather than resorting to force and power.

Even High Mountains Will Collapse If Dug at Daily

高山也要垮，如果每天挖

Indonesia

This proverb means that friendships need careful maintenance; if not preserved and continually damaged, even the strongest bonds will eventually collapse. Similar Chinese proverbs include "A thousand-mile dike can be destroyed by an ant's nest," indicating that small, neglected issues can lead to significant problems, emphasizing the importance of maintaining relationships and preventing minor damages.

Without Mutual Understanding, Deep Friendship Cannot Be Established

没有相互了解，就不能建立深厚情谊

Brunei

On November 17, 2018, on the eve of his state visit to Brunei, President Xi Jinping published a signed article titled "Jointly Writing a New Chapter in China-Brunei Relations" in the *Borneo Bulletin*, *See Hua Daily News*, *United Daily News*, and *Sin Chew Daily*. The article quoted this Bruneian proverb: "Without mutual understanding, deep friendship cannot be established." Chinese people say, "True acquaintance lies in mutual understanding." In the article, President Xi stated, "We are willing to be sincere friends and good partners for mutual development with Brunei. I believe that with the joint efforts of our governments and peoples, the friendly cooperative relationship between China and Brunei will write an even more beautiful chapter."

This widely circulated proverb in Brunei illustrates the importance of communication and understanding in building deep friendships. Brunei and China, friendly neighbors across the sea, have had mutual exchanges since the Western Han dynasty (202 BC–AD 8) through the Maritime Silk Road, creating a beautiful chapter of mutual acquaintance and kinship. Regarding the development of China-Brunei relations, President Xi Jinping noted in the article, "The Belt and Road Initiative I proposed has received positive responses and strong support from Brunei. Both sides signed a memorandum of understanding to align this initiative with Brunei's 'Vision 2035,' injecting new momentum into the development of bilateral relations."

Today, the joint construction of the Belt and Road by Brunei and China has yielded fruitful results, with major projects and cooperation platforms like Hengyi Brunei Petrochemical and the "Guangxi–Brunei Economic Corridor" playing active roles in promoting Brunei's economic diversification, becoming vital drivers of Brunei's economic growth.

3

The People Are the Foundation of the Nation; When the Foundation Is Strong, the Nation Is Peaceful

Introduction

The Chinese proverb, "The people are the foundation of the nation; when the foundation is strong, the nation is peaceful," emphasizes the idea that the people are the fundamental basis of the country; when the foundation is solid, the nation can be stable and peaceful. China's whole-process people's democracy is fundamentally based on prioritizing the people and serving them wholeheartedly.

Achieving national prosperity and continuously improving the material and spiritual living standards of the people, as well as fulfilling their aspirations for a better life, are the urgent demands and common wishes of all Chinese people. To achieve these goals, it is essential to rely on the collective efforts of all people and mobilize their enthusiasm. Practice has shown that democracy is historical and specific, and can be chosen in various forms and content. It is not limited to the Western-style democracy that claims to represent the entirety of democratic practice. In a rapidly changing world, most developing countries find it difficult to alter their national and ethnic destinies by simply copying Western political systems.

China's democracy always puts the people's interests first. To protect and realize these interests, the CPC leads the people in constantly improving democratic systems, enriching democratic forms, and broadening democratic channels, thereby expanding orderly political participation at all levels and in all fields. As a result, people's democracy has become more extensive, ample, and robust, exhibiting vibrant vitality.

Under the leadership of the CPC, the Chinese people have truly become the masters of their country. Over the years, with the continuous advancement and improvement of whole-process people's democracy, the Chinese people have not only enjoyed more extensive, ample, and comprehensive democratic rights, but China has also established the world's largest education system, social security system, and healthcare system. The quality of life for the people has significantly improved, and the nation has achieved unprecedented development miracles.

The People Are the Foundation of the Nation; When the Foundation Is Strong, the Nation Is Peaceful

民惟邦本, 本固邦宁

China

"The people are the foundation of the nation; when the foundation is strong, the nation is peaceful" is a crucial concept in ancient Chinese political civilization. Traditional people-centered thought embodies the essence of benevolent governance, improving people's livelihood, and promoting societal stability. Today, we have fully absorbed the wisdom of traditional people-centered thought and made significant advancements in its content, institutional guarantees, and practical outcomes, genuinely enabling the people to be the masters of their country, achieving a historic height in the democratic process of the Chinese nation.

This proverb carries the political wisdom of successive Chinese sages. "The people are the source of power"; truly understand the people's will; "what the people desire, do well, and what the people despise, avoid"; genuinely practice "caring for the people's concerns"; "use power for the people"; and "seek benefits for the people." These are all critical contributions of contemporary China to global democratic politics.

The People Are Precious, and the Ruler Is Light

民为贵，君为轻

China

This proverb comes from *Mencius*, originally stating, "The people are precious, the altars of the gods of earth and grain are secondary, and the ruler is light." It means that "the people are the most important, the gods of earth and grain come next, and the ruler's position is the least important." Mencius proposed this significant idea, suggesting that the establishment of a country requires people, and only with a country does the need for a ruler arise. Mencius positioned the relationship between the ruler, the state, and the people by using their relative importance. His people-centered thought is a gem in the history of ancient Chinese philosophy.

The tradition of people-centered thought has a long history, originating in the Xia, Shang, and Zhou periods (c. 2070–256 BC), with extensive discussions in pre-Qin literature. Represented by Confucius and Mencius, the Confucian school proposed the idea of the people as the main body, forming a comprehensive and rich people-centered thought system. Mencius's viewpoint that "the people are precious" recognized the people's dominant role in society, although he did not find the means or measures to realize this position under the historical conditions of his time. Hence, ancient people-centered thought was more of a political ideal of the ancient sages.

In the new era, General Secretary Xi Jinping has creatively proposed a people-centered development ideology based on inheriting traditional people-centered thought. He has enriched and developed China's people-centered thought from multiple theoretical and practical perspectives, achieving a significant advancement over traditional Confucian people-centered thought.

When the Big River Is Full, the Small Rivers Are Full; When the Small Rivers Are Full, the Big River Is Full

大河有水小河满，小河有水大河满

China

This proverb uses the flow of river water to illustrate the interdependence between different rivers. Sometimes it is written as "When the big river is full, the small rivers are full; when the small rivers are full, the big river is full," and sometimes as "When the big river is full, the small rivers are full; when the big river is dry, the small rivers are dry," implying that neither the big river nor the small rivers can exist independently, and their destinies are closely linked.

In his keynote speech at the Boao Forum for Asia Annual Conference 2015 on March 28, 2015, President Xi Jinping stated, "To move toward a community of shared destiny, we must adhere to win-win cooperation and common development. Friends in Southeast Asia say, 'When the water rises, the lotus flowers grow.' Friends in Africa say, 'If you want to go fast, go alone; if you want to go far, go together.' Friends in Europe say, 'A single tree cannot block the cold wind.' The Chinese say, 'When the big river is full, the small rivers are full; when the small rivers are full, the big river is full.' These all convey the same principle: only through cooperation and win-win can we accomplish great, good, and lasting endeavors."

On October 14, 2021, in his keynote speech at the opening ceremony of the Second United Nations Global Sustainable Transport Conference, President Xi Jinping pointed out, "When the small rivers are full, the big river is full; when the big river is dry, the small rivers are dry. Only through openness, inclusiveness, and connectivity can countries help each other and achieve mutual benefit. We must promote the building of an open world economy, avoid discriminatory and exclusive rules and systems, and promote economic globalization toward a more open, inclusive, balanced, and win-win direction."

Water Can Carry a Boat and Also Capsize It

水能载舟，亦能覆舟

China

This proverb likens the people to water and the rulers to boats, meaning that water can support a boat to sail smoothly, but it can also capsize it.

"Water can carry a boat and also capsize it" originally comes from *Xunzi · The Regulations of a King* (荀子·王制): "The ruler is the boat; the common people are the water. The water can carry the boat, and the water can capsize the boat." Xunzi reiterated this point in *Xunzi · Duke Ai* (荀子·哀公), emphasizing the relationship between the ruler and the people, expressing his political thought of "loving the people" vividly. Wei Zheng of the Tang dynasty (AD 618–907) also mentioned in "Ten Thoughts of Emperor Taizong": "Resentment is not great, but people are fearful; water carries and capsizes the boat, and this should be deeply cautious." This phrase is a well-known truth among Chinese people.

In 2016, General Secretary Xi Jinping quoted this proverb in his speech at the commemoration of the 80th anniversary of the victory of the Long March of the Red Army, stating, "'Water can carry a boat and also capsize it.' This truth must be remembered; we must never forget it. The people are the heavens, and the people are the earth. Forgetting the people and losing touch with them will make us like water without a source and a tree without roots, leading to failure."

A Sage Has No Fixed Will; He Takes the Will of the People as His Own

圣人无常心，以百姓心为心

China

Ancient Chinese sage Laozi wrote in the *Tao Te Ching* (道德经): "A sage has no fixed will; he takes the will of the people as his own," meaning that a sage does not have a fixed and unchanging will but should follow and respect the will of the people. This does not imply that a sage lacks opinions, but rather that a sage should adhere to and respect the people's wishes.

When Xi Jinping was the Secretary of the Zhejiang Provincial Committee, he quoted "A sage has no fixed will; he takes the will of the people as his own" in his 2007 article "The Relationship between Master and Servant Must Not Be Reversed," urging "leading cadres at all levels to always start from the people's interests and stand on the people's stance in life, work, and governance." Since the 18th National Congress of the CPC, General Secretary Xi Jinping has frequently used "taking the will of the people as one's own" to explain the CPC's commitment to seeking happiness for the Chinese people. He emphasized, "In the process of comprehensively deepening reform, we must adhere to the Marxist view of the masses and the party's mass line, 'taking the will of the people as our own,' and make the realization, maintenance, and development of the fundamental interests of the broadest masses of the people the starting point and goal of promoting reform, allowing development results to benefit all people more equitably." In 2019, Xi Jinping pointed out: "Taking the will of the people as our own, breathing the same air, sharing the same fate, and being heart-to-heart with the people, is the CPC's original intention and eternal commitment."

Good Cinnabar Needs No Paint to Be Red

好的朱砂不用涂色也红

Thailand

The Lao proverb, "Good cinnabar does not need to be painted red," mirrors the Chinese sayings, "A house with a phoenix tree will naturally attract phoenixes," "Musk deer naturally emit fragrance without needing to stand in the wind," and "Good wine needs no bush." These proverbs suggest that if a person has true talent or a thing possesses excellent quality, its reputation will naturally spread without the need for self-promotion.

Water Depends on the Boat; the Tiger Relies on the Forest

水依船, 虎靠林

Thailand

This proverb means that water and boats are mutually dependent, as are tigers and forests, akin to the relationship between the government and the people, similar to "Water can carry a boat and also capsize it." In the natural environment, things are interconnected and coexistent; similarly, in the international community, partners and neighbors must rely on each other for mutual support and coexistence.

In the new context, China regards ASEAN as a priority direction for its peripheral diplomacy and a key region for high-quality Belt and Road cooperation. This will bring more opportunities for exchanges and cooperation in economic, political, social, and cultural development between China and ASEAN countries. China and ASEAN countries are close neighbors with interconnected bloodlines. Since the establishment of dialogue relations in 1991, both sides have worked hand in hand, mutually achieving success and setting a model for regional common development and win-win cooperation.

The Stability of Officials' Desks and Chairs Does Not Depend on Nails and Mortises

官吏桌椅稳不稳,并不在于钉和榫

Laos

This Lao proverb reminds officials to consider the welfare of the people, as the stability of an official's position depends not on nails and mortises but on the people's support. If officials do not work for the people's benefit, their positions will not last.

In Laos, there are many proverbs that express hopes and warnings for leaders. "When you ride an elephant and become a king, do not forget the farmers riding buffaloes and carrying seedlings," which urges rulers not to forget the common people; "When you ride a white elephant, do not hold your head high and laugh arrogantly, as the elephant palanquin may stumble," which advises officials not to be arrogant; "If you wear official robes and become a king, do not forget the common folk in the valleys," which reminds officials always to keep the people in mind.

One Stick of Wood Does Not Make a Fire; One Stick of Wood Does Not Make a Fence

一柴燃不起大火，一木围不成篱笆

Laos

One stick of wood cannot kindle a big fire, and one stick of wood cannot form a fence. Human society is a community of shared destiny, requiring mutual understanding and support. President Xi Jinping has frequently elaborated on the concept of a community with shared future for humanity at major international events and time points, earning widespread acclaim and recognition from the international community.

Asia has always played an important role in promoting global development and shaping new economic and political mutual trust. The important foundation supporting Asia's development is the friendly cooperation and mutual exchange in various fields between China and ASEAN countries.

Plant Mulberry Trees When You Can; Mend Fences When You Leave

在时种桑树，走时修篱笆

Laos

This Lao proverb means that one should always do good deeds, avoid laziness, and be diligent, ensuring that tasks are continuously attended to, earning respect and affection from others. Hard work and friendliness are valuable human values that should be promoted in international politics, making them a global consensus. Facing the wave of globalization, China's proposal to build a community with shared future for mankind captures the vision of "peace, development, cooperation, and win-win outcomes" for the world. For the entire world, we should embrace the spirit of "breathing the same air, sharing the same fate," and strive to "plant mulberry trees when we can, and mend fences when we leave," making our world a better place.

Good Rice Grows Because of Ditches

水稻长得好,是因为有水沟

Laos

The development of a country depends on whether the people support it and whether their enthusiasm is mobilized. These require norms for protection, as anything needs norms to ensure good distribution and assistance, helping things develop better. Rice needs ditches to grow well, allowing water to flow properly to each field to avoid droughts and floods. The role of ditches is significant; they are like the people's will. Things align with the people's will, just as water flows smoothly. Rice receives enough water, and grows prosperously.

Aim High, but Be Down-to-Earth

想,要凌云壮志;干,要脚踏实地

Myanmar

This proverb from Myanmar emphasizes the need to have lofty ideals while also possessing the practical spirit of working step by step. Transforming grand strategic goals into reality requires practical, down-to-earth methods. The Chinese say, "Plan for difficulty when it is easy; work on the great while it is small. Difficult tasks in the world must be done when easy; great tasks must be done in detail," and "Slow to speak but quick to act," highlighting the importance of determination and practicality.

In his speech at the 60th anniversary of the Five Principles of Peaceful Coexistence in 2014, President Xi Jinping quoted the ancient Chinese saying, "A journey of a thousand miles begins with a single step," and the proverb from Myanmar, "Aim high, but be down-to-earth," both expressing the aspiration to work with the international community to build a harmonious world of lasting peace and common prosperity.

"Enduring the splendor of heaven and earth, human endeavors arise from hardships." The more beautiful the future is, the more it requires our hard work and efforts.

Even Buddha Cannot Go against the Will of Monks; a Leader Cannot Go against the Will of People

佛祖难违众僧意，领袖难违众民心

Myanmar

Myanmar is a multi-ethnic country, with each ethnic group having its own language, and some even having their own script. Proverbs in Myanmar are rhythmic, melodious, easy to remember, and concise yet profound in meaning. "Even Buddha cannot go against the will of monks; a leader cannot go against the will of people" reflects Myanmar's social reality, indicating that even in areas where Buddhism is prevalent, Buddha must consider the opinions of ordinary monks. In the political field, it means that leaders must listen to the voice of the people and cannot be dictatorial, autocratic, or self-willed.

A Good Tree Brings a Whole Forest

一棵好树带来全林

Myanmar

This proverb emphasizes the valuable influence and impact of good examples and outstanding individuals on the whole. Currently, both China and Myanmar face the significant task of developing the economy, improving people's livelihoods, and leading the people toward a happy and beautiful life. Under the framework of the Belt and Road Initiative, the two countries are jointly building the China–Myanmar Economic Corridor, implementing Chinese aid projects, and focusing on supporting the development of agriculture, water conservancy, education, and healthcare to enhance people-to-people friendship. Cultivating good trees one after another will inevitably bring fields of fragrance to both countries.

4

Forging Iron Requires a Strong Hammer

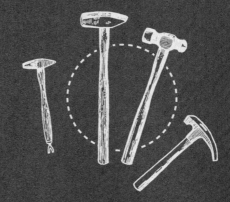

Introduction

In today's world, many countries have adopted Western-style "election" systems. Some of these countries have operated such systems for a long time, yet their economic development is far from satisfactory, and the improvement of people's lives has been slow and ineffective. In some nations, the introduction of Western political systems has not led to the expected checks and balances or clean governance. Instead, it has resulted in parties sabotaging each other, increased backdoor dealings, and more severe corruption, making economic development and the improvement of living standards even harder to achieve. Under Western political systems, existing social and political divisions in some countries have been deliberately magnified, leading to splits and exacerbating previously resolved ethnic, religious, economic, and political conflicts. This disruption has broken the peace of people's lives, and some nations have even fallen into turmoil and conflict. Over one hundred countries worldwide have adopted Western political systems. If such systems could truly lift a nation from poverty and weakness, leading to development and a higher quality of life, there would be more developed countries in the world today.

Ultimately, for a country to achieve development and prosperity and bring tangible benefits to its people, it must firmly follow its path without being misled by superficial political and economic phenomena from the West. This is the essence of "forging iron requires a strong hammer." Development must follow a path that suits the country's own conditions.

Forging Iron Requires a Strong Hammer

打铁还需自身硬

China

This proverb means that when forging iron, the hammer used must be strong enough to shape good tools. Forging involves repeatedly hammering raw materials on an anvil until they are shaped, so both the anvil and the hammer must be harder than the raw materials. The extended meaning is that one must have the strength and capability to accomplish tasks and that one should hold oneself to high standards before expecting the same from others.

Qian Qi, a politician in the Ming dynasty (AD 1368–1644) wrote in *Qian Gongliang Ce Yu* (钱公良测语): "Those who govern others must first govern themselves; those who demand accountability from others must first hold themselves accountable; those who achieve must first achieve themselves." This saying emphasizes the extreme importance of the personal qualities of those in power.

Hands Not Rowing, Rather Feet Blocking the Water

手不摇橹，却拿脚挡水

Thailand

This proverb means that someone not only fails to help but also makes obstacles, similar to the Chinese saying, "not rowing the boat but putting one's feet in the water." Similar proverbs exist in Vietnam and Laos, such as "If you do not row, do not put your feet in the water," warning against behaviors that cause trouble.

The ancient civilizations of Asia have fostered a spirit of inclusivity and coexistence. Despite differences in political systems and development paths, Asian countries share similar views on democracy and values. Democracy is a universal human value, and there is no single model of democracy suitable for all countries. Democracy is not the exclusive patent of Western countries, and actions that undermine the democratic development of regional nations for selfish reasons are unacceptable.

Kicking One's Own Leg

摇足就刺

Thailand

This proverb means to bring trouble upon oneself, similar to the Chinese saying "lifting a rock only to drop it on one's own foot." This simple yet profound and concise proverb is commonly used in ASEAN countries, encapsulating local wisdom to accurately and vividly criticize self-inflicted suffering. The Vietnamese proverb, "The belly does the work, but the belly bears the consequences," also carries the meaning of "reaping what one sows."

Some Western countries have tried to interfere in the internal affairs of others, only to end up damaging their own credibility and ruining international relations, thus falling into their own trap. "Kicking one's own leg" aptly describes such behavior.

A Dog Barking at a Dry Banana Leaf

狗吠干芭蕉叶

Thailand

This proverb is used to describe someone who talks but does not act, likened to a dog barking at a dry banana leaf. Thai people use this real-life event to symbolize empty talkers who make a lot of noise without taking any action.

Forcing a Cow to Eat Grass by Pushing Its Horns

按牛角强迫其吃草

Thailand

This Thai proverb means forcing someone to do something they are unwilling to do. Whether a cow eats grass should be the cow's decision, not something enforced by external force. Such coercion often backfires, even if well-intentioned. The proverb advises respecting others and natural laws rather than imposing one's will on others. Similar Chinese sayings include "forcing a cow to drink water" and "a forcefully picked melon is not sweet." Vietnamese proverb, "forcing a cat to eat ginger," and Lao proverb, "a cow is forced to eat grass by pushing its horns, and its horns will break; a pig is beaten to eat bran, its snout will raise," convey the same meaning.

In ASEAN countries, animals like water buffaloes, elephants, dogs, chickens, and fish are frequently used in proverbs, reflecting the close relationship between these animals and the people's natural environment, production, lifestyle, and cultural customs. These animal-related proverbs provide insights into local living conditions, attitudes toward nature, society, life, and governance, reflecting their democratic values and practices.

A Lizard Obtains Gold

蜥蜴得了黄金

Thailand

This proverb describes someone who, upon receiving wealth or status, becomes arrogant and forgets themselves, akin to the Chinese saying "a vile person intoxicated by success." This Thai proverb uses a metaphor to convey profound meanings and serves as a warning to others.

The saying originates from the Thai literary work—*A Lizard Obtains Gold*. Lizards are nimble and swift creatures common in tropical regions. Due to their small size, they are very cautious. However, when they gain something beyond their capacity, they often lose control and become overly proud.

In Thai folklore, this proverb is used to criticize low-status or morally inferior individuals who, upon gaining something good, become conceited and reveal their true, ugly nature. The similar proverb, "becoming proud like a bull forgetting its legs," highlights criticism and satire.

Eat Dog Food and Become a Dog;
Eat Cat Food and Become a Cat

吃狗饭变成狗,吃猫饭变成猫

Vietnam

This common Vietnamese proverb suggests that one's companion influences one's character, similar to the saying, "You become wise by associating with the wise, and foolish by associating with fools." The Thai proverb "Follow a demon and become a demon; follow a ghost and become a ghost," the Chinese proverb "One who stays near vermilion gets stained red; one who stays near ink gets stained black," and the Lao proverb "Enter a vulture flock and become a vulture; enter a crow flock and become a crow" all express the same idea. They emphasize that a good companion can make a person better, while a bad companion can make a person worse, highlighting the impact of the environment on individuals.

China and ASEAN countries share close geographical ties and have made continuous progress in strengthening strategic communication, deepening exchanges in various fields, and developing comprehensive strategic cooperative partnerships. All countries should strive to create a harmonious environment that fosters closer and friendlier regional economic cooperation.

The Egret Finds Food, and the White Crane Enjoys It

鹭鸶觅食，白鹤享用

Vietnam

This Vietnamese proverb criticizes those who gain without laboring, benefiting from others' efforts.

Egrets and white cranes are common in Southeast Asia. People generally admire egrets and attribute them with positive qualities. A Lao proverb says, "Live like a food-seeking egret; when soaring, be as bright as a cattle egret." Egrets have slender bodies and graceful plumes. They often stand on one leg in the water, using their sharp beaks to fish. They can break open clams by throwing them onto rocks. White cranes often live in the same areas as egrets, and people use white cranes to criticize those who unfairly benefit from others' labor. The Chinese idiom, "The pigeon occupies the magpie's nest," has a similar meaning. Such behavior of seizing others' labor fruits and destroying others' happiness has always been despised.

Throwing a Stick beyond the Mango Tree

越过芒果甩出棍

Laos

This proverb means criticizing others without reflecting on one's own faults or going to unnecessary lengths. Thailand has a similar proverb. Since the establishment of ASEAN, member countries have maintained peaceful and friendly relations. In foreign relations, ASEAN has not only maintained good relations with regional powers but also established a comprehensive set of Asia-centric regional mechanisms and frameworks, showcasing its unique role in regional diplomacy and cooperation.

Eating at Someone's House and Defecating on Their Roof

在别人家中吃饭，往别人屋顶拉屎

Laos

This proverb criticizes forgetting the kindness of others and acting against them. Thailand has a similar saying, "Eating in the house and defecating on the roof," condemning such behavior.

In international relations, some act with gratitude, while others are ungrateful and treacherous. The behavior of "eating at someone's house and defecating on their roof," disregarding international ethics, will ultimately be condemned and abandoned by the international community.

Curled-Horn Bulls Like to Fight; Rogues Like to Cause Trouble

卷角牛好打架，无赖汉好找茬

Laos

In Laos, curled-horn bulls represent stubborn and unreasonable people, similar to rogues who disrupt social order by fighting and causing trouble, making them unwelcome.

Rogue behavior in international relations often causes great anger. Some countries engage in rogue actions, breaking promises, applying double standards, acting hegemonically, and becoming "curled-horn bulls" and "rogues" on the international stage.

The Eye Can See Everything but Itself

人眼能见一切物，唯独不见自己眼

Laos

The eye is one of the most important human organs, providing over seventy percent of external information. However, even such a crucial organ has its limitations—it cannot see itself. This proverb illustrates that no one is perfect and everything has flaws. The greatest shortcoming is the inability to see one's own image and recognize one's defects.

Chinese wisdom advocates self-reflection through mirrors: "With a bronze mirror, one can straighten clothes and hats; with a history mirror, one can understand rise and fall; with a people mirror, one can see gains and losses."

Vultures Do Not Fly with Eagles; Golden Phoenixes Do Not Fly with Snake Eagles

秃鹫不跟苍鹰飞，金凤不与蛇雕飞

Laos

This Lao proverb means that people with different principles do not work together, similar to the Chinese saying "Birds of a feather flock together." It implies that only those with the same values can unite to achieve great things. Those who are motivated by selfish interests and follow a different path cannot be true friends.

The border areas between China and ASEAN countries, such as Vietnam, Laos, and Myanmar, are gateways from China to the Indochina Peninsula and hubs for Southeast Asian economic and trade cooperation. Residents on both sides of the border maintain social interactions and mutual support through production, daily life, and festival rituals. This continuous interaction helps shape a multi-dimensional identity system, fostering stability and good neighborly relations in border regions.

Pushing a Stone Mortar up a Mountain

滚石臼上山

Laos

This proverb means attempting something beyond one's abilities, similar to the Chinese saying "An ant trying to shake a tree" and the Thai saying "Pushing a stone roller up a mountain," all expressing the idea of overestimating oneself. As we know, a stone mortar is extremely heavy, making it impossible to push uphill alone. This proverb uses exaggeration to convey the speaker's negative view.

In international affairs, the core of leadership should be based on moral justice, supported by comprehensive national strength. However, some superpowers, relying on their military and economic might, arbitrarily threaten others with force and interfere in other countries' internal affairs, losing moral standing. Even as their power and resources decline, they refuse to adapt to changes, still trying to "push a stone mortar up a mountain."

A Hen Clucks All Day but Can Only Lay One Egg

母鸡咯咯叫一天还是只能生一个蛋

Myanmar

This Myanmar proverb uses the example of a hen to satirize those who do little but make a big fuss, seeking recognition and praise. The Lao proverb, "The hen that lays the egg is the one that clucks," conveys a similar meaning. For hens, clucking after laying an egg is a natural behavior, but in human society, excessive self-promotion is unwelcome.

After the 2008 global financial crisis, many economies struggled, and the negative spillover effects of developed countries' monetary policies led to secondary shocks for emerging economies. Meanwhile, rising unilateralism further exacerbated the global governance crisis. In such a context, merely clucking like a hen without seeking to establish fair and effective rules to address international issues will ultimately be abandoned by the world.

Urging a Cow to Give Birth

催牛生产

Brunei

This Brunei proverb satirizes actions that go against natural laws and are impatient for success, similar to the Chinese saying "pulling up seedlings to help them grow." Acting against natural laws always leads to undesirable results and may even cause harm to others.

Don't Blame the Floor for Being Uneven If You Can't Dance

不会跳舞不要怪地板不平

Brunei

This proverb ridicules those who lack ability but blame their surroundings and external conditions for their failure, using excuses to absolve themselves of responsibility.

Since the end of the Cold War, under the constructed "universal values" narrative by some Western capitalist countries, China and ASEAN countries have long been suppressed and discriminated against by some countries. With China becoming the world's second-largest economy and the rapid development of ASEAN countries, some Western countries fear their interests and international status are threatened, leading them to further smear China and try to draw in some ASEAN countries.

We need to clearly understand the international environment, effectively use media power, construct a sound narrative, tell China's story well, and strengthen China–ASEAN exchanges. By showcasing the good lives of the people, we can break down slanders and enhance mutual understanding in various fields.

A Civet Cat Covered in Chicken Feathers

插着鸡毛的狸猫

Indonesia

This proverb satirizes those who lack substance but put on the air. Similar to the Chinese saying, "The fox assuming the majesty of the tiger," it describes people who borrow others' power or prestige to benefit themselves.

The Frog under the Coconut Shell Thinks the Sky Is Only That Big

椰壳下面趴着的青蛙认为天就那么大

Indonesia

This Indonesian proverb, like the Thai "The frog under the coconut shell," is equivalent to the Chinese saying, "A frog in a well." It describes someone with a narrow perspective who is unaware of the broader world outside their limited environment.

Saving a Handful of Salt Spoils a Whole Ox

姑息一撮盐，烂了一头牛

Indonesia

The Lao proverb, "Willing to kill an ox, but reluctant to spend a handful of salt," also describes people who lose big over small things. It's similar to the idiom "penny-wise and pound-foolish," illustrating the folly of being stingy over minor things while losing significant ones.

If You Are Not Upright, You Mislead Others

自身不正，教人误听

Singapore

This Singaporean proverb means that if you cannot conduct yourself properly, you should not mislead others. It advises ignoring those who criticize others without acknowledging their own weaknesses. Singapore is a multi-ethnic society dominated by Chinese culture, with many proverbs similar to Chinese ones. The Chinese often say that one should lead by example and set a precedent to inspire others.

The Belt and Road Initiative proposed by China in 2013 has moved from concept to implementation. In promoting the initiative, international trade rules have played an irreplaceable role in coordinating interests, reducing conflicts, and achieving win-win outcomes. The initiative has always emphasized diversified participation, development-oriented goals, and the ultimate pursuit of a community with shared future for mankind. These new development concepts centered on win-win cooperation have promoted the construction of international trade rules, embodying Chinese wisdom and principles, which differ fundamentally from the objectives of Western-developed countries.

Frequent Lies Ruin One's Reputation

谎话说多，人格扫地

Cambodia

This proverb means that someone who frequently lies will lose the trust of others and no one will listen to them anymore. Similar to the Chinese fable "The Boy Who Cried Wolf," if one always deceives others, no one will come to help when genuine trouble arises. In international affairs, lies are also ineffective. Interactions between countries should be based on principles of honesty, trust, mutual benefit, and common development to achieve a shared future.

The international economic order established by Western countries after World War II does not represent the interests of developing countries, featuring unfair benefit distribution and governance failures. Currently, emerging economies like China are rapidly developing and have a vested interest in improving global rules, seeking fairer and more just international norms

Grab a Snake by Its Neck, or It Will Bite Back

捉蛇要紧握蛇脖子，否则蛇会转过头来咬人

Cambodia

This proverb advises that one should not be lenient with bad people and must seize their weak points, just as catching a snake requires holding it by the neck to prevent it from biting back. The Chinese fable "Mr. Dongguo and the Wolf" similarly teaches not to be merciful to evildoers. This Cambodian proverb warns us to be vigilant and prevent bad people from retaliating.

Frequent Lies Ruin One's Reputation

谎话说多，人格扫地

Cambodia

This proverb means that someone who frequently lies will lose the trust of others and no one will listen to them anymore. Similar to the Chinese fable "The Boy Who Cried Wolf," if one always deceives others, no one will come to help when real trouble arises. In international affairs, lies are also ineffective. Interactions between countries should be based on principles of honesty, trust, mutual benefit, and common development to achieve a shared future.

The international economic order established by Western countries after World War II does not represent the interests of developing countries, featuring unfair benefit distribution and governance failures. Currently, emerging economies like China are rapidly developing and have a vested interest in improving global rules, seeking fairer and more just international norms.

5

Many Hands Make Light Work; Many Stakes Make a Strong Fence

Introduction

Under the framework of the Global Civilization Initiative, China and ASEAN countries continue to develop while jointly and steadfastly defending the principles of democratizing international relations. They are unwavering builders of world peace, contributors to global development, and defenders of international order, promoting shared human values. The spirit of mutual assistance in Chinese culture extends to foreign exchanges, closely related to the historical traditions and development process of Chinese civilization.

The distinct geographical features of China—its vast rivers, mountains, plains, and rivers—have been a crucial natural foundation for the unity and cohesion of Chinese civilization. The story of Yu the Great's Flood Control exemplifies the spirit of unity and cooperation. Managing floods requires a collective effort, highlighting not just the practical methods of flood control but, more deeply, the spirit of organizing people effectively to work together, strive against nature, and change their destiny.

Different regions, ethnic groups, and their histories, traditions, and customs shape different civilizations, which in turn shape their views of civilization. The view of civilization formed in

China's modernization process is one of equality, mutual learning, dialogue, and inclusiveness. It advocates that different civilizations should coexist harmoniously, complementing each other, and that civilization exchanges should surpass barriers, mutual learning should overcome conflicts, and coexistence should transcend superiority.

Human society is facing increasingly severe environmental crises. In such a situation, international cooperation is essential. Countries should respect and tolerate each other, and embrace the world's diversity. China and ASEAN countries should work together to seek common ground while preserving differences, complement each other's strengths, and strive for harmonious coexistence and win-win cooperation.

One Fence Needs Three Stakes; One Hero Needs Three Helpers

一个篱笆三个桩，一个好汉三个帮

China

This proverb means that an individual's strength is limited, but with the help of others, tasks can be accomplished more effectively.

Whether in economic trade or political cooperation, going it alone is unwise. "One fence needs three stakes; one hero needs three helpers." Having trustworthy and supportive partners helps one achieve greater success.

In the trade exchanges between China and Belt and Road countries, ASEAN countries, especially Singapore, Malaysia, Indonesia, Vietnam, Thailand, and the Philippines, play a crucial role. The partnership between China and ASEAN countries has proven to be mutually beneficial, significantly contributing to regional development.

Peach and Plum Do Not Speak, yet a Path Is Made Beneath Them

桃李不言，下自成蹊

China

The original meaning of this proverb is that peach and plum trees do not speak, but because their flowers are beautiful and their fruits delicious, people flock to pick them, thus creating a path beneath the trees. It means that sincere and honest people naturally win others' hearts. This saying first appeared in *Records of the Grand Historian · Biographies of General Li* (史记·李将军列传), "I have seen General Li, humble and modest like an ordinary person, unable to speak eloquently. When he died, both those who knew him and those who didn't mourned deeply. His loyalty and integrity deeply touched scholars and officials. The saying goes, 'Peach and plum do not speak, yet a path is made beneath them.' This small saying can be applied to larger matters."

In his speech at the opening ceremony of the 2017 Belt and Road Forum for International Cooperation, President Xi Jinping mentioned, "In the autumn of 2013, I proposed the Silk Road Economic Belt and the 21st Century Maritime Silk Road—collectively known as the Belt and Road Initiative—in Kazakhstan and Indonesia. 'Peach and plum do not speak, yet a path is made beneath them.' In the past four years, more than one hundred countries and international organizations have actively supported and participated in the Belt and Road Initiative, with important resolutions from the United Nations General Assembly and the Security Council incorporating it. The Belt and Road Initiative has moved from concept to action, from vision to reality, yielding fruitful results."

The Chinese people value "practice" and "effectiveness," believing that justice naturally resides in people's hearts. The significant achievements of the Belt and Road Initiative since its proposal and its contributions to global development are self-evident.

Live in Harmony with All Neighbors and Avoid Gossip

和所有的邻居和睦相处,不说闲话

Thailand

Neighbors live close to us, and in times of difficulty, they are the first to extend a helping hand. Neighbors should assist each other and avoid causing disputes. Disputes with neighbors should be resolved amicably, with mutual respect and understanding. Chinese culture values humility, advocating "yielding three feet to avoid conflict," always cherishing the friendship between neighbors.

Cultural beliefs play a significant role in bridging social conflicts. Harmonious relationships based on cultural mutual trust help maintain political stability and social harmony in the region.

A Single Line Does Not Make a Rope; a Single Tree Does Not Make an Orchard

单线不成绳,独树不成果园

Vietnam

This proverb means that one person alone cannot achieve much, similar to the Chinese saying, "One cannot clap with one hand." It emphasizes the importance of teamwork and collaboration.

China and ASEAN countries are economically interdependent, especially evident in the economic field. Currently, the economic development levels of various countries differ significantly, with many developing countries at the early or accelerating stages of industrialization and urbanization. There are considerable differences and complementarities in economic and trade development among these countries, necessitating enhanced cooperation for mutual development.

A Stick Supports the Banana Stalk, and the Banana Stalk Supports the Stick

木棍支蕉秆，蕉秆撑木棍

Laos

This proverb means that people need to support each other, just like how a banana stalk needs a stick to stay upright, and the stick needs the banana stalk to stand firm.

Strengthening cooperation between China and ASEAN countries showcases both cultural uniqueness and commonality, transcending narrow nationalism. It reflects the historical ties of friendly exchanges and mutual support among the peoples of China and ASEAN countries, embodying the diverse, coexisting, and interactive cultural ecology of China–ASEAN relations. With the establishment of the China–ASEAN comprehensive strategic partnership and the official implementation of the Regional Comprehensive Economic Partnership, China continues to expand high-level openness, actively promoting deep integration between the Chinese economy and the global economy. Along with ASEAN countries, China shares development opportunities with the world, exemplified by the mutual support of "a stick and a banana stalk."

Good Trees Need Leaves; Gentlemen Need Friends

佳木要有叶，君子要有朋

Laos

This Lao proverb means that good trees need green leaves to flourish, just as virtuous people need friends.

In the current international landscape, where global structures are undergoing profound adjustments, China provides tremendous stability and injects strong positive energy into the global pursuit of a better future, making it a good friend to people worldwide. Amidst unprecedented global changes, China's economic development serves as a stable factor in an uncertain environment.

Unity Is the Source of Happiness; Division Is the Fountain of Destruction

团结是幸福之源，分裂是灭亡之泉

Laos

This proverb stresses the importance of unity. Unity ensures survival, while division leads to destruction. No matter how strong something is, it can still encounter a more formidable force.

In the face of unforeseen difficulties and dangers, only by uniting and concentrating strength can people overcome challenges, while division leads to danger and misfortune. Unity is humanity's inevitable choice in the face of fate and an effective way to deal with risks.

Tigers Hunt Because the Forest Is Dense, and the Forest Thrives Because Tigers Reside

虎捕猎物因林密，林茂因有虎栖息

Laos

This proverb illustrates the mutual dependence between tigers and forests: tigers can catch prey because the forest is dense, and the forest maintains ecological balance and lushness because tigers hunt herbivores. Everything in this world is interdependent and cannot exist in isolation.

The concept of a community with shared future for mankind contains the essence of Chinese traditional "harmony" culture and adopts a non-violent approach to foreign relations. Guided by Marxist theory, it incorporates and draws upon the rational elements of Chinese traditional culture, inheriting and developing China's diplomatic philosophy, thereby enhancing the persuasiveness and explanatory power of the concept. The fate of all peoples is interconnected; no country can or should achieve its security at the expense of others. Countries should actively participate in global security governance to achieve common, comprehensive, cooperative, and sustainable security. Just like the saying, "Tigers hunt because the forest is dense, and the forest thrives because tigers reside," we live in the same "forest" bound by shared destiny.

A Nation without United Hearts Cannot Prosper

民心不齐国不盛

Laos

This Lao proverb emphasizes the importance of collective unity, asserting that a nation must unite to thrive, similar to the Chinese saying, "When people are of one mind, they can turn the earth into gold." The Chinese also value unity, as recorded in *The Book of Changes* (易经): "When two people are of one mind, their sharpness can cut through metal; when their words are in harmony, their scent is like orchids." This saying evolved in daily use to that "when brothers are united, their sharpness can cut through metal," meaning that when people are united like brothers, they can unleash incredible power.

Many Stakes Make a Strong Fence; Many Hands Make Light Work

桩多篱笆牢，人多好办事

Laos

This proverb means that many stakes make a fence strong, and many people make work easier. Unity is strength. The Chinese say, "When people are united, they can move Mount Tai." When everyone works together with a common goal, no obstacle is insurmountable, and no challenge is too difficult to overcome.

The Lao proverb expresses that unity and cooperation bring strength and success, emphasizing the importance of working together for mutual benefit.

The Entire Village Drinks from One Well and Walks on One Path without Treading on Each Other's Footprints

全村所有人，共饮一井水，同走一条道，互不踩脚印

Laos

Laos, located at the junction of tropical and subtropical regions with high mountains, dense forests, and abundant rainfall, has many proverbs related to water, forests, and tropical plants. These proverbs, using metaphor, reflect Laos cultural characteristics and contain stories, legends, and myths. This proverb uses a well and a path as metaphors to indicate that people should live in harmony, respect each other, and build a shared community.

Lao traditional moral values highly emphasize human relationships, believing that collective strength surpasses individual power. Achieving unity requires people not to undermine or disparage each other, just as walking on the same path means not stepping on each other's footprints.

Grasp Today to Not Lose Tomorrow

抓住今天，才能不丢失明天

Philippines

This proverb means that seizing present opportunities prevents missing future development prospects. The international situation changes rapidly, and opportunities are fleeting. Countries must seize development opportunities now to ensure a better future.

Currently, the world is undergoing significant changes, entering a new era of great development and transformation. Multi-polarity, economic globalization, information society, and cultural diversity continue to advance, and global governance systems and international order are undergoing transformation. The interdependence among countries has deepened significantly, leading to a stronger call for peace and sustainable development in the international community.

You Reap What You Sow

种什么树就结什么果

Philippines

This proverb means that outcomes depend on the causes, the same as the Chinese saying, "You reap what you sow." In international affairs, only by treating neighbors and friends with sincerity and kindness can one achieve harmony and assistance.

This principle is essential for "sowing good seeds to reap good fruits" and building a peaceful, harmonious international society. It embodies the democratization of international relations.

The More You Visit Relatives and Friends, the Closer You Get

亲戚越走越亲，朋友越走越近

Myanmar

This Myanmar proverb means that the more often relatives and friends visit and communicate, the closer their relationship becomes. The same applies to the interaction between countries.

On January 17–18, 2020, President Xi Jinping paid a state visit to Myanmar. On the eve of the visit, Xi Jinping published a signed article titled "Writing a New Chapter in the Millennia-Old Pauk-Phaw Friendship" in Myanmar's *Myanmar Alin*, *Mirror*, and *Myanmar Global New Light* newspapers. At the end of the article, Xi Jinping emphasized, "Both China and Myanmar have a saying, 'The more you visit relatives and friends, the closer you get.' Standing at the new historical starting point of the 70th anniversary of diplomatic relations, we are willing to work hand in hand with Myanmar friends to build a closer China-Myanmar community with shared future and write a new chapter in the millennia-old Pauk-Phaw friendship."

Scattered Cows Fall Prey to Tigers; Disunited People Suffer Heavy Losses

牛群涣散进虎口，人不团结受重创

Myanmar

If a herd of cows is not united and scattered like a loose sandpile, they will fall prey to tigers. Similarly, people who are not united will face strong enemies and suffer heavy losses.

The rapid development of Asia in recent decades can be attributed to the unity, mutual help, and open cooperation among countries, embracing and promoting the trend of global economic development. Without unity, each country would become isolated islands, and human civilization, economic development, and political enlightenment would lose vitality and opportunities for growth and prosperity.

The Chinese saying, "In and out, we help each other; in times of trouble, we watch out for each other," reflects the idea that people should support and live harmoniously with each other.

Honest Advice Is Hard to Take, Just as Straight Trees Are Hard to Climb

忠言逆耳，直树难攀

Myanmar

This proverb means that honest and sincere advice is often hard to hear, just as climbing a straight tree is difficult. It suggests that we should have an open and inclusive attitude, being able to listen to sincere and well-intentioned words, even if they are hard to hear.

The Chinese saying "Good medicine is bitter to the mouth but good for the disease; honest advice is unpleasant to the ear but beneficial for conduct" carries a similar meaning. This also highlights the similarities and closeness between many traditional values in Myanmar and China.

Even the Tallest Pagoda Must Start from the Ground

再高的宝塔也得从地起

Indonesia

This proverb means that the tallest pagoda is built from the ground up, emphasizing that no matter how great the endeavor is, it must be started from the basics and built up gradually with hard work. Chinese proverbs, "Gathering sand to build a tower" and "A thousand-mile journey begins with the first step," imply that without practical and diligent work, grand dreams cannot be realized.

In 2013, during his speech at the Indonesian Parliament, President Xi Jinping quoted "A tree as big as a man's embrace grows from a tiny sprout; a nine-storied tower rises from a heap of earth" from *Tao Te Ching*, explaining that "to keep the tree of China–ASEAN friendship evergreen, we must solidify the social foundation of bilateral relations," which shares the same meaning as the Indonesian proverb.

Conclusion

The world is rich and colorful. The splendid Chinese civilization and the diverse Southeast Asian civilizations have formed a profound and bright Eastern civilization through thousands of years of exchanges.

Civilization is always reflected in people's daily life, and proverbs express various aspects of life in simple and popular forms. Proverbs reflect philosophical thoughts, have educational functions, and summarize the experiences and wisdom of generations.

In March 2023, China issued the Global Civilization Initiative, which, together with the Global Development Initiative and the Global Security Initiative, becomes one of the three solid pillars supporting the community with shared future for mankind. Under the guidance of the Global Civilization Initiative and the vision of building a community with shared future for mankind, China promotes the democratization of international relations to build a new type of international relations and uphold shared human values of peace, development, fairness, justice, democracy, and freedom. This embodies Chinese wisdom and solutions for the progress of human political civilization and reflects universal global values.

Chinese-style modernization has created a new form of human political civilization. Its successful practice has contributed to Chinese wisdom and experience in the world. The leadership of the Communist Party of China has enabled the Chinese people to become masters of their country, creating the miracle of Chinese governance. Chinese-style modernization has great significance domestically and internationally, shaping a new global civilization. It boosts the confidence of developing countries in independent development and provides a new path for those aspiring to achieve autonomous development.

The successful practice of Chinese-style modernization is the first of its kind among non-Western, non-capitalist Eastern countries, achieving autonomous, endogenous development without colonial exploitation, ethnic enslavement, or foreign invasion wars. This modernization breaks through the logic of Western capital domination and foreign hegemony, pursuing mutual benefit and common development, highlighting moral superiority. Chinese-style modernization has opened a unique and effective development path in the history of world politics.

China not only finds its own successful path but is also willing to work with ASEAN countries and other countries to create prosperity together. President Xi Jinping emphasized that China is willing to work with ASEAN countries to grasp the trend, eliminate interference, share opportunities, and create prosperity. By implementing the comprehensive strategic partnership, both sides are taking new steps toward building a closer China–ASEAN community with shared future. Together, we will build a peaceful, secure, prosperous, beautiful, and friendly home.

References

Deng, Shubi, and Hui Peng. *Selected Cambodian Proverbs* (柬埔寨谚语选编). Beijing: Foreign Language Teaching and Research Press, 2023.

Guo, Sijiu, and Xueliang Tao. *Cham* (查姆). Kunming: Yunnan People's Publishing House, 2018.

He, Shengda. *History of Cultural Development in Southeast Asia* (东南亚文化发展史). Kunming: Yunnan People's Publishing House, 2010.

Ji, Chang. *The Book of Changes* (周易). Translated and annotated by Yang Tiancai and Zhang Shanwen. Beijing: Zhonghua Book Company, 2011.

Laozi. *Tao Te Ching* (道德经). Translated and annotated by Jing Zhang and Songhui Zhang. Beijing: Zhonghua Book Company, 2021.

Li, Xiaoyuan, and Liangmin Zhang. *Selected Lao Proverbs* (老挝语谚语选编). Beijing: Foreign Language Teaching and Research Press, 2021.

Mengzi. *Mencius* (孟子). Translated and annotated by Yong Fang. Beijing: Zhonghua Book Company, 2017.

Valmiki. *Ramayana* (罗摩衍那). Translated by Xianlin Ji. Changchun: Jilin Publishing Group, 2021.

Wolfgang, Mieder. *Folkloristic Study of Proverbs* (谚语的民俗学研究). Translated by Zhang Juwen. Beijing: China Social Sciences Press, 2022.

Yang, Lizhou. *Translation and Annotation of Thai Proverbs* (泰国谚语译注). Chongqing: Chongqing University Press, 2015.

ABOUT THE EDITOR

Feng Yue is a researcher at the Institute of Political Science, Chinese Academy of Social Sciences, and the Deputy Secretary-General of the Chinese Red Culture Research Association. His primary research interests include comparative studies of political and historical development between China and the West, and grassroots Party building and governance in China.